GRENADA TRAVEL GUIDE 2023

*Grenada Unveiled: The Perfect Island Getaway -An
Exploration of History, Culture, Cuisine And Natural
Wonders*

Amanda D. Gideon

Table Of Contents

Introduction
History of Grenada
Geography And Climate
15 Facts About Grenada
Reasons Why You Should Visit Grenada
Population of Grenada
The Language of Grenada

Chapter 1: Planning Your Trip
How To Get To Grenada
Best Places To Stay In Grenada
Best Hotels In Grenada
Accommodation and Prices
Transportation Options and Prices
Best Time To Visit Grenada
Tips To Enjoying Grenada
Entry and Visa requirements

Chapter 2: Exploring Grenada
Top Attractions In Grenada
Things To Do And See In Grenada
Outdoor Activities In Grenada
Shopping and Souvenirs In Grenada
Popular Shopping Areas In Grenada
Local Products and Souvenirs
Entertainment And Nightlife In Grenada.
Best Beaches And Resorts In Grenada

Chapter 3: Cultural and Culinary Experiences
Culture And Traditions Of Grenada
Festivals and Events In Grenada
Grenada Foods And Drinks You May Try
Local Markets And Street Food
Best Restaurants In Grenada
Useful Phrases And Vocabulary

Chapter 4: Practical Information
Safety Tips And Precautions
Health Considerations
Local Customs And Etiquette
Currency And Money Matters
Time Zone and Public Holidays
How To Save Money On Grenada Vacation
Do's And Don'ts In Grenada

Conclusion

Introduction

Welcome to the pleasant island country of Grenada! Grenada is a captivating blend of natural beauty, a long history, and a vibrant culture that can be found in the southern Caribbean. Known as the "Spice Isle" because of its bountiful creation of nutmeg, cinnamon, and different flavors, this tropical heaven allures explorers with its unblemished sea shores, lavish rainforests, and warm cordiality. Grenada's vibrant towns, mouthwatering cuisine, and captivating heritage are all part of the experience. Grenada is a magical getaway that will captivate you, whether you're looking for adventure or relaxation.

History of Grenada

Grenada is a picturesque nation of islands in the Caribbean Sea that has a fascinating, centuries-long history. Prior to the arrival of European settlers, the island's indigenous people were known as the Caribs.

During his third voyage to the Americas, Christopher Columbus made a stop in Grenada in 1498. However, it wasn't until 1650 that the French established a permanent presence on the island.

Throughout the 17th and 18th centuries, the British and French fought for Grenada's control. The Deal of Paris in 1763 at long last conceded the island to England, laying out Grenada as an English settlement.

Grenada became a significant sugar producer under British rule, heavily dependent on slave labor. The island's economy shifted to the production of cocoa and nutmeg following the abolition of slavery in the 19th century.

In 1974, Grenada acquired freedom from England and turned into an established government inside the Federation. Political flimsiness followed, prompting an upset in 1979 when the left-wing New Gem Development, driven by Maurice Priest, assumed command.

Minister laid out a communist Leninist government and formed close bonds with Cuba and the Soviet Association. Nonetheless, inward divisions inside the decision party prompted a battle for control, bringing about the shocking occasion known as the "Grenadian Unrest."

In 1983, an overthrow inside the New Gem Development brought about the execution of the Head of the State Maurice Minister and a few individuals from his administration. Following this rough occasion, the US, alongside Caribbean countries, sent off Activity Earnest Anger, attacking Grenada to reestablish request and vote-based administration.

Grenada returned to democratic rule following the intervention, enjoying stability and progress ever since. The country's economy has enhanced, zeroing in on the travel industry, farming, and seaward money.

Grenada is still a stunning destination that is well-known for its beautiful beaches, lush rainforests, and friendly people. It likewise assumes a functioning part in territorial and foreign relations as an individual from the Caribbean People Group (CARICOM) and the Unified Countries.

Geography And Climate

Grenada is a volcanic island in the Caribbean Ocean, found north of Trinidad and Tobago. It is the Windward Island with the most southerly slope. With a total area of 344 square kilometers, the island is approximately 34 kilometers long and 14 kilometers wide.

A central mountain range that runs north-south through the island's center dominates Grenada's geography. The most noteworthy point is Mount St. Catherine, which is 2,757 feet (840 meters) tall. The island also has a number of smaller mountains, valleys, and rivers.

The environment of Grenada is tropical, with warm temperatures and high stickiness. There are few seasonal variations in the temperature, which hovers around 28°C (82°F) on average. The wet season runs from June to December, with a normal of 150 inches (3,810 millimeters) of precipitation each year. The dry season, which lasts from January to May, brings an annual rainfall average of 60 inches (1,500 millimeters).

Timber, tropical fruit, and deepwater harbors are Grenada's natural resources. The island is likewise a significant maker of nutmeg, cocoa, and bananas.

Grenada is a well-known traveler location, with delightful sea shores, rich rainforests, and various verifiable and social attractions. The Grenada National Park, which safeguards a variety of animal and plant species, is also located on the island.

15 Facts About Grenada

The following are 15 top realities about Grenada:

1. Grenada is a nation of islands in the southeast of the Caribbean Sea.

2. It is frequently alluded to as the "Spice Isle" because of its plentiful creation of flavors like nutmeg, cloves, and cinnamon.

3. St. George's, Grenada's largest city and capital, is also the island's capital.

4. The official language of Grenada is English, mirroring its pioneer history.

5. Grenada acquired freedom from English rule on February 7, 1974.

6. Warm temperatures and a rainy season from June to November characterize the island's tropical climate.

7. Excellent Etang Public Park, situated in the focal point of the island, is home to the shocking Terrific Etang Lake and rich rainforests.

8. Grenada is renowned for its wonderful white-sand sea shores and completely clear waters, drawing in vacationers from around the world.

9. The country is made up of three fundamental islands: Grenada, Carriacou, and Unimposing Martinique.

10. In 1983, Grenada stood out as truly newsworthy when the US and Caribbean countries sent off a tactical mediation following an upset and political flimsiness.

11. Grenada's Carnival is a well-known cultural festival marked by lively parades, music, and dancing.

12. Oil down and callaloo soup are two examples of the island's diverse cuisine, which is influenced by African, Indian, and European culinary traditions.

13. Grenada's high-quality chocolate is made possible by the country's reputation for producing some of the finest cocoa beans in the world.

14. The leatherback sea turtle, an endangered species, lives on Grenada's seashores during the settling season.

15. Grenada is a Commonwealth of Nations member with Queen Elizabeth II as head of state, who is accompanied by a Governor-General.

Reasons Why You Should Visit Grenada

Grenada offers a different scope of attractions and encounters that make it an optimal objective to visit. Here are a few convincing motivations to investigate this delightful Caribbean island:

1. Amazing Regular Excellence: From lush rainforests and cascading waterfalls to pristine beaches with crystal-clear waters, Grenada has stunning landscapes. The pleasant view makes a peaceful and relaxing climate.

2. Island Spice: Known as the "Flavor Island," Grenada is popular for its fragrant nutmeg, cinnamon, cloves, and different flavors. The island's rich spice production history can be learned about by visiting spice plantations.

3. Warm and Inviting Society: The agreeable local people in Grenada cause guests to feel comfortable. Music, dance, and festivals on the island all reflect the island's vibrant culture, offering a delightful immersion into the Caribbean way of life.

4. Submerged Wonderland: The island offers magnificent jumping and swimming open doors. Grenada's immaculate coral reefs and wrecks furnish an energetic submerged world overflowing with marine life, making it a heaven for jumpers and sea lovers.

5. Grenadian Food: Experience the island's exceptional culinary enjoyments, mixing Caribbean, African, and French impacts. Try Grenada's national dish, "oil down," as well as the island's fresh seafood and tropical fruits.

6. Memorable Locales and Design: The island's numerous forts, museums, and vibrant colonial-era buildings let you learn about its fascinating past. Find out about Grenada's past and the way that it assumed a pivotal part in the Caribbean's verifiable setting.

7. Experience Exercises: For the brave on a fundamental level, Grenada offers exercises like climbing through rainforests, investigating the Great Etang Public Park, and leaving on exciting zip-line visits.

8. Loosening up Sea shores: Grenada has more than 40 beautiful beaches where you can unwind and enjoy the sun. There is a spot for everyone who enjoys the beach, whether it's Bathway Beach, Grand Anse Beach, or Morne Rouge Bay.

9. Responsible Travel: Grenada is dedicated to sustainable tourism and the preservation of its cultural and natural heritage. Guests can participate in eco-accommodating exercises and backing nearby organizations that focus on mindful practices.

10. Escape from the Groups: Dissimilar to some other famous Caribbean objections, Grenada remains moderately uncrowded, giving a more close and legitimate travel insight.

In outline, Grenada offers an ideal mix of regular excellence, warm friendliness, social lavishness, and courageous open doors, making it a charming objective for explorers looking for a genuine Caribbean experience.

Population of Grenada

As of July 2023, it is anticipated that 126,183 people will live in Grenada. The population is

371.13 individuals per square kilometer, which makes Grenada quite possibly the most thickly populated country in the Caribbean. The capital and biggest city is St. George's.

Most of the inhabitants in Grenada are of African drop, with a critical minority of European, East Indian, and blended heritage. The authority language is English, however, most of the populace likewise speaks Grenadian Creole, a French-based Creole language.

The middle age in Grenada is 31.6 years. The populace is developing at a pace of 0.7% each year, which is somewhat underneath the normal for the Caribbean district. The fruitfulness rate is 2.1 youngsters per lady, which is simply beneath the substitution pace of 2.1.

Tourism, agriculture, and light manufacturing drive Grenada's economy. With roughly 25% of GDP, tourism is the largest economic contributor. Horticulture is the second biggest donor, representing around 15% of the Gross domestic product. The vital farming items are nutmeg, mace, cocoa, and bananas. Light assembling is likewise a significant piece of the economy, with the fundamental items being clothing, furniture, and drugs.

Grenada is an individual from the Caribbean People Group (CARICOM) and the Association of American States (OAS). The nation is likewise a Federation domain, with Sovereign Elizabeth II as the head of state.

The Language of Grenada

The authority language of Grenada is English, yet the vitally communicated language is both of two Creole dialects: Grenadian Creole French or "patois," and occasionally Grenadian Creole English.

Grenada is home to a Creole language known as "Grenadian Creole English." The Southern branch of English-based Eastern Atlantic Creoles includes it. The majority of Grenada's inhabitants speak it, which is a blend of African, French, and English.
A variant of Antillean Creole is Grenadian Creole French. It is spoken by a little minority of the inhabitants in Grenada, chiefly in the rustic regions. It is a combination of French, English, and African dialects.

In everyday conversation, as well as in some forms of literature and music, Grenadian Creole English and Grenadian Creole French are used. English is utilized in government, schooling, and business.

The utilization of Creole dialects in Grenada is an impression of the island's set of experiences and culture. The French first colonized Grenada in the 17th century, and the British followed in the 18th. The amalgamation of the languages spoken by the African slaves brought to the island and those spoken by the French and British colonists led to the development of the Creole languages.

Grenada's Creole languages are a vibrant and significant component of the island's culture. They are a source of pride for the people of Grenada and a way for Grenadians to express their identity and heritage.

Here are a few instances of words and expressions in Grenadian Creole English:

A person from Grenada is called a "**Bajan**." "**Fam**" means family,
 "**Livity**" means way of life,
"**Noh bad**" means no problem, "**Sweetness**" means something good or nice,
"**Wuk**" means work,
 "**Yuh**" means you.

If you're going to Grenada, it's helpful to know some basic words and phrases in Grenadian Creole English. This will assist you with speaking with local people and getting around the island.

Chapter 1: Planning Your Trip

Arranging a tour to Grenada can be an interesting and remunerating experience! Here are some fundamental stages to assist you with arranging your excursion:

1. Research and Pick Dates: Start by exploring the best opportunity to visit Grenada in light of your inclinations for climate and exercises. Take into consideration any local festivals or events you would like to attend.

2. Book Flights and Convenience: When you have your movement dates, book your trips to Maurice Priest Global Air terminal. Then, at that point, pick facilities that suit your financial plan and inclinations. Grenada offers a scope of choices, from extravagant retreats to comfortable guesthouses.

3. Make a plan of action: Based on your interests, plan your daily activities and sightseeing. Take in the island's historic sites, waterfalls, lush rainforests, and stunning beaches. Remember to incorporate time for unwinding and partaking in the neighborhood food.

4. Spending plan and Cash: Lay out a financial plan for your excursion and get to know the Eastern Caribbean Dollar (XCD), Grenada's true cash. Keep in mind that not all establishments may accept credit cards, so bring some cash.

5. Pack as needed: Pack light and bring suitable dress for the heat and humidity. Remember basics like sunscreen, bug repellent, and any essential meds.

6. Find out about Culture and Customs: To show respect to the locals and ensure a more immersive experience, familiarize yourself with Grenadian culture and customs.

7. Travel Protection: Think about buying travel protection that covers health-related crises, trip abrogations, and any likely unexpected conditions.

8. Actually look at Visa Prerequisites: Check in the event that you want a visa to enter Grenada in light of your ethnicity, and guarantee your identification is substantial for no less than a half year past your movement dates.

9. Health Warnings: Counsel your PCP about suggested immunizations and wellbeing safeguards prior to making a trip to Grenada.

10. Transportation: Research transportation choices inside Grenada. Taxis, rental vehicles, and neighborhood transports are normal strategies for getting around the island.

11. Remain Refreshed on Tourism warnings: Check for any tourism warnings or updates connected with Grenada to remain informed about wellbeing and security during your outing.

Make sure to be adaptable and open to new encounters during your excursion. Grenada's regular magnificence, amicable local people, and energetic culture make certain to make it an extraordinary experience!

How To Get To Grenada

There are multiple ways of getting to Grenada. The most widely recognized way is via plane, as there are non-stop departures from many significant worldwide urban communities. The fundamental air terminal in Grenada is Maurice Diocesan Global

Air terminal (GND), which is found right beyond the capital city of St. George's.

Here is a portion of the carriers that fly to Grenada:

American Airlines, Delta, Virgin Atlantic, Air Canada, British Airways, JetBlue Airways, Caribbean Airlines, LIAT, SVG Air, and interCaribbean Airways are among the airlines that offer flights to the Caribbean from the United States. London, Frankfurt, and Paris are typically the destinations of European flights.

In the event that you are going from a more modest city or island, you might have to interface through a significant air terminal. For instance, assuming you are going from Los Angeles, you should associate through Miami or New York.

You can get around Grenada by taxi, bus, or renting a car once you arrive. Taxis are the most advantageous method for getting around, however, they can be costly. Transports are a less expensive choice, yet they are not as regular. If you intend to explore a lot, renting a car is a good option.

Here are other ways of getting to Grenada:

Journey ship: A few journey lines offer travels that stop in Grenada. This is a wonderful way to see the island and learn about the culture there.

Ferry: There are ships that run between Grenada and Carriacou, an adjoining island. This is an extraordinary method for seeing the two islands.

Private boat: You can sail to Grenada if you have your boat. The island can be explored at your own pace with this method.

Best Places To Stay In Grenada

Grenada, also known as the "Spice Isle," has a wide range of stunning lodging options, each with its special charm. The best choices are as follows:

1. Great Anse Ocean side: In the event that you love the ocean side, remaining at a retreat or inn along the Fabulous Anse Ocean side is an ideal decision. You'll have simple admittance to the delicate white sands and perfectly clear waters, alongside a scope of water sports and close by conveniences.

2. St. George's: The capital city, St. George's, offers a blend of facilities, including store inns, guesthouses, and beguiling overnight boarding houses. It's a phenomenal area for investigating authentic destinations, nearby business sectors, and the beautiful harbor.

3. Dainty Anse Sound: For a more segregated encounter, consider remaining close to Modest Anse Sound. This region gives quiet settings, lovely perspectives, and an opportunity to loosen up encompassed commonly.

4. National Park of Levera: Nature sweethearts will value remaining close to Levera Public Park. The park is well-known for its stunning beaches, wildlife, and (seasonally) the chance to see sea turtle nests.

5. Plantations of spices: Stay at one of the traditional spice plantations to immerse yourself in Grenada's aromatic spice culture. These remarkable lodgings offer a brief look into the island's set of experiences and culinary customs.

6. Carriacou: Carriacou, one of Grenada's sister islands, offers a quieter and more authentic island experience. You'll track down beguiling guesthouses and houses with dazzling perspectives on the Caribbean Ocean.

7. Real Blue: Honest to Goodness is a lively region with a blend of facilities, including store lodgings and condos. The Molinere Underwater Sculpture Park's captivating underwater sculptures and St. George's University are both within close proximity.

While arranging your visit to Grenada, think about your inclinations, spending plan, and wanted encounters. Whether you favor ocean front extravagance, personal guesthouses, or vivid nature withdraws, Grenada brings something to the table for each explorer.

Best Hotels In Grenada

Here are probably the best lodgings in Grenada, in light of their surveys and appraisals on TripAdvisor:

Silversands Grenada is an extravagant ocean front hotel with shocking perspectives on the Caribbean Ocean. It has different eateries, bars, and pools, as well as a spa and a wellness community.

Shoes Grenada is another comprehensive retreat that is ideally suited for couples. It has 10 eateries, 6 bars, 4 pools, and an elite spa.

Radisson Grenada Ocean side Resort is a more reasonable choice that is as yet situated on a lovely ocean side. It has 2 eateries, 2 bars, and an outside pool.

Calabash Luxury Boutique Hotel is a small, cozy hotel that focuses on pampering and relaxation. It has a spa, a wellness community, and a housetop pool with staggering perspectives.

Mount Cinnamon Resort and Ocean Side Club is a family-accommodating hotel with different exercises and conveniences. It has 4 cafés, 3 bars, 4 pools, and a water park.

These are only a couple of the numerous extraordinary lodgings in Grenada. You are certain to find the ideal lodging on this beautiful island, regardless of your interests or budget.

Accommodation and Prices

These are some examples of Grenada's lodging options and prices:

Budget:

Jewel Occasion Ocean Side Resort: This ocean front retreat has cooled rooms with kitchenettes, a café, a bar, and a porch. The nightly rates start at around $100.

Wave Crest Holiday Apartments: These condos are situated in Amazing Anse, near the ocean side. They have completely prepared kitchens, and some have galleries with ocean sees. Costs start from $120 each evening.

Mid-range:

Mount Cinnamon Grenada: This extravagant resort has 4 eateries, 4 bars, a spa, and a tennis court. Costs start from $250 each evening.

Calabash Extravagance Store Hotel: This shop lodging is situated in St. George's, and has 12 rooms, an eatery, a bar, and a roof porch with staggering perspectives on the city. Costs start from $300 each evening.

Shoes Grenada: This comprehensive hotel has 10 eateries, 5 bars, a spa, and different exercises. Costs start from $500 each evening.

Silversands Grenada: This comprehensive hotel has 5 eateries, 4 bars, a spa, and a title green. Costs start from $600 each evening.

These are only a couple of models, and there are numerous other extraordinary spots to remain in Grenada. The prices are just a guide, and they may change depending on when and where rooms are available.

Transportation Options and Prices

Here is a portion of the transportation choices accessible in Grenada, alongside their costs:

Taxis: Taxis are the most well-known method for getting around Grenada. They are metered, however, the rates can shift contingent upon the hour of the day and the distance voyaged. A common taxi passage from the air terminal to Excellent Anse Ocean side would cost around $15 USD.

Bus: There is a public transport framework in Grenada that is moderately reasonable. Transports run consistently between the significant towns and towns, and the tolls are truly reasonable. A one-way transport ticket from St. George's to Fabulous Anse Ocean side would cost around $1 USD.

Ferry: There are likewise ships that run between the various islands of Grenada. The ships are an extraordinary method for getting around to investigate the various pieces of the island. A one-way ship ticket from St. George's to Carriacou would cost around $10 USD.

Vehicle rental: If you have any desire to have greater adaptability and investigate the island at your own speed, you can lease a vehicle. There are a few vehicle rental organizations in Grenada, and the rates differ contingent upon the sort of vehicle you lease and the period of time you lease it for. A normal day to day vehicle rental rate would cost around $50 USD.

Water taxi: Water taxis are an extraordinary method for getting around the Terrific Anse region. They are a touch more costly than the transports, yet they are a lot quicker and more helpful. A one-way water taxi ticket from Stupendous Anse Ocean side to Morne Rouge would cost around $5 USD.

The most effective way to go around Grenada relies upon your spending plan and your inclinations. On the off chance that you are on a careful spending plan, the transport or the ship are the most ideal choices. In the event that you need greater adaptability, you can lease a vehicle or take a taxi. Additionally, a water taxi is an excellent choice if you want to explore the Grand Anse region.

Additional pointers for getting around Grenada include the following:

- Obtain an international driver's license if you intend to rent a vehicle.

- On the off chance that you are taking a taxi, make certain to settle on the charge before you get in the vehicle.

- The transport framework in Grenada isn't generally dependable, so it is smart to have a fall back in the event that you are anticipating taking the transport.

- The ships are an extraordinary method for getting around, yet they can be packed during busy times.

- Assuming you are anticipating doing any climbing or investigating in the rainforest, make certain to wear solid shoes and bring a lot of water.

Best Time To Visit Grenada

Grenada is a stunning island in the Caribbean that has a lot to offer visitors. The weather conditions are warm and radiant all year, yet there are two particular seasons: the dry season (January to May) and the stormy season (June to December).

The dry season is the best chance to visit Grenada if you have any desire to stay away from the downpour and partake in the most daylight. The typical temperature during this time is 84°F to 86°F, with highs of up to 90°F. There is a normal of 2 to 3 crawls of downpour each month during the dry season.

The following are some of the advantages of visiting Grenada during the dry season:

- **Fewer people:** The dry season is the pinnacle season for the travel industry in Grenada, however, the groups are as yet more modest than in other Caribbean objections.

- **Clear skies:** The skies are clear and radiant most days during the dry season, making it ideal for ocean side exercises, climbing, and touring.

- **Lower costs:** Costs for flights, inns, and exercises are by and large lower during the dry season.

If you want to see the island's lush rainforests and have a more affordable vacation, 'the rainy season' is a good time to visit Grenada. The typical temperature during the stormy season is 82°F to 84°F, with highs of up to 90°F. There is a normal of 6 to 8 creeps of downpour each month during the blustery season.

A portion of the advantages of visiting Grenada during the stormy season include:

- **Lower costs:** Costs for flights, lodgings, and exercises are for the most part lower during the blustery season.

- **Fewer groups:** The stormy season is the slow time of year for the travel industry in Grenada, so there are fewer groups at the sea shores, cafés, and vacation spots.

- **Lavish rainforests:** The blustery season is an extraordinary chance to investigate

Grenada's lavish rainforests, which are home to various plants and creatures.

Other considerations when selecting a time to visit Grenada include:

The Spicemas (Carnival) festival takes place in August, the Grenada Sailing Festival takes place in January and February, and the Carriacou Maroon and Indigenous Festival takes place in February. Assuming you're keen on going to one of these occasions, you'll have to as needs be plan your excursion.

Typhoon season: Grenada is situated in the storm belt, so there is a gamble of typhoons from June to November. However, for more than two decades, the island has not been directly affected by a hurricane. You might want to steer clear of Grenada at this time if you are worried about hurricanes.

At last, the best opportunity to visit Grenada relies upon your own inclinations. If you have any desire to keep away from the downpour and partake in the most daylight, the dry season is the best opportunity to go. The rainy season is a good time to go to the island if you want to see the lush rainforests and have a cheaper vacation.

Tips To Enjoying Grenada

To appreciate Grenada, think about these tips:

1. Investigate the Sea shores: Grenada has beautiful beaches. For stunning sand and crystal-clear water, go to Bathway Beach, Grand Anse Beach, and Morne Rouge Beach.

2. Jump into Submerged Magnificence: The island offers fabulous swimming and jumping open doors. Find bright marine life and investigate wrecks.

3. Adventure in the Spice Market: Explore the bustling markets and inhale the distinctive aroma of Grenada's nutmeg and cinnamon.

4. Cascade Pursuing: Annandale Falls and Seven Sisters are two cascading waterfalls that are ideal for refreshing dips and tranquil views.

5. Experience Nearby Cooking: Attempt conventional dishes like Oil Down (stew) and callaloo soup at nearby eateries and food slows down.

6. Flavor Ranches: Take a visit through zest manors to find out about the island's flavor creation and history.

7. Island Bouncing: Consider bouncing to local islands like Carriacou and Modest Martinique for an alternate encounter.

8. Drink Local Rum: Test a portion of Grenada's brilliant rums at refineries like Stream Antoine and Clarke's Court.

9. Take part in Celebrations: Assuming your visit concurs with one, drench yourself in the lively climate of celebrations like Spicemas Fair.

10. Nature Journeys: Visit Grand Etang National Park and take in the breathtaking views as you hike through the rainforest.

Make sure to regard nearby traditions and customs, and forever be aware of ecological preservation during your visit. Have fun while you're in Grenada!

A Sample Itinerary For Vacation In Grenada

Without a doubt, here's an example schedule for an outing in Grenada:

Day 1:

- Show up in Grenada and look into your convenience.
- -Unwind and loosen up on one of the lovely sea shores, like the Excellent Anse Ocean side.
- Partake in a delectable supper at a nearby café to test Grenadian food.

Day 2:

- Take a morning climb to the Annandale Cascades and partake in the rich environmental elements.
- -Visit the Grenada Public Exhibition hall to find out about the island's set of experiences and culture.
- -At night, investigate the lively air of St. George's, the capital city.

Day 3:

- Go to the submerged model park at Molinere Inlet for a remarkable swimming encounter.
- -Visit Post George for shocking all encompassing perspectives on the island and the harbor.

- Partake in a few shopping at the nearby business sectors for keepsakes and specialities.

Day 4:
- Set out on a day visit to the shocking Excellent Etang Public Park, home to the Stupendous Etang Lake and various natural life.
- Take an invigorating swim at the Seven Sisters Cascades.
- At night, attempt some nearby road food at the Gouyave Fish Friday celebration.

Day 5:
- Go on a boat visit to investigate the delightful encompassing islands, like Carriacou or Modest Martinique.
- Partake in some water sports exercises like kayaking, paddleboarding, or cruising.
- Experience a loosening up dusk journey to end the day.

Day 6:
- Visit the memorable Belmont Bequest, a functioning ranch with cocoa and zest creation.

- Take a directed visit to find out about the island's farming and enjoy a chocolate-production studio.
- In the early evening, unwind at La Sagesse Ocean Side and Nature Save.

Day 7:
- Go through the morning at Levera Ocean side and partake in the tranquil environmental elements.
- Visit the Levera Public Park to notice settling ocean turtles (occasionally, normally from April to October).
- Leave from Grenada with brilliant recollections of your excursion.

Kindly note that this is only a recommended schedule and can be redone in view of your inclinations and the term of your visit. Partake in your excursion in Grenada!

Entry and Visa requirements

Here are the passage and visa prerequisites for Grenada as of August 2023:

Visa requirements: Grenada is open to tourists from most nations without requiring a visa. Be that as it may, there are a couple of exemptions, like residents of Pakistan, India, and Bangladesh. These residents should apply for a visa ahead of time.

Identification validity: Beyond the duration of your planned stay in Grenada, your passport must be valid for at least six months.

Section requirements: At the point when you show up in Grenada, you should introduce your identification, a return or forward ticket, and verification of adequate assets to help your visit. You may likewise be approached to give a medical coverage declaration.

Visa on arrival: A visa can be obtained upon arrival in Grenada from certain nations, including China, India, and Pakistan. In any case, this is dependent on future developments, so it is in every case best to check with the Grenada Migration Office before you travel.

Chapter 2: Exploring Grenada

Grenada, frequently alluded to as the "Zest Isle," is a charming Caribbean objective eminent for its rich scenes, beautiful sea shores, and dynamic culture. Investigating Grenada offers a superb encounter, incorporating a rich embroidery of regular miracles and verifiable fortunes.

One of the features of a visit to Grenada is its perfect sea shores. Terrific Anse Ocean side, a dazzling two-mile stretch of fine white sand, is a number one among voyagers looking for unwinding and watersports. For a more detached vibe, make a beeline for Levera Ocean side or Morne Rouge Ocean side, where you can lounge in serenity in the midst of stunning landscape.

Nature devotees will be captivated by Grenada's verdant rainforests and flowing cascades. Climbing through Amazing Etang Public Park permits you to observe the island's assorted verdure, including the subtle Mona monkeys. The recreation area's focal point, the cavity pool of Stupendous Etang, offers a quiet spot to mull over the magnificence of nature.

Grenada's spice industry assumes a critical part in its legacy, visiting the nutmeg handling stations and flavor cultivates an unquestionable requirement. The island's fiery smell swirls into the atmosphere as you find out about the development and handling of cinnamon, cloves, and, obviously, nutmeg.

To dive into Grenada's set of experiences and culture, investigate the capital city, St. George's. The horseshoe-formed harbor is embellished with bright structures, a conspicuous element of the pleasant Carenage. Visit Stronghold George for all encompassing perspectives on the city and the encompassing shore.

Food aficionados will get a kick out of Grenada's scrumptious cooking, imbued with flavors from the island's multicultural legacy. Try not to miss attempting the public dish, Oil Down, a flavorful one-pot feast consisting of breadfruit, meat, coconut milk, and flavors.

Grenada is additionally known for its lively celebrations and occasions. The vivacious Festival, held in August, grandstands beautiful processions, calypso music, and abundant road parties that commend the island's extraordinary character.

Whether you are looking for a laid-back ocean side get-away, an eco-experience, or a social inundation, investigating Grenada offers a paramount encounter that will leave you charmed and yearning to return.

Top Attractions In Grenada

Grenada, also known as the "Spice Isle," is a popular Caribbean destination known for its stunning natural beauty and rich cultural heritage. Here are a portion of the top attractions you should investigate while visiting Grenada:

1. Beach Grand Anse: This notorious ocean side is one of the most lovely in the Caribbean, flaunting completely clear waters, delicate white sands, and a pleasant scenery of rich green slopes. It's a great spot for water sports, sunbathing, and swimming.

2. Saint George's The capital city of Grenada: St. George's, is a beguiling and vivid town with a memorable stronghold, delightful harbor, and interesting roads fixed with frontier time design. Make certain to visit Stronghold George for amazing perspectives on the city and encompassing regions.

3. Falls in Annandale: A characteristic miracle found simply a short drive from St. George's, Annandale Falls is a beautiful cascade encircled by rich tropical vegetation. It's a famous spot for swimming and drenching yourself in nature.

4. Submerged Model Park: Off the coast of Molinere Bay, Grenada is home to the first underwater sculpture park in the world. The recreation area includes an assortment of novel figures that have become counterfeit reefs, making it an entrancing spot for swimming and jumping.

5. Falls of Seven Sisters: Seven Sisters Falls, a series of cascading waterfalls in the rainforest, is a tranquil and refreshing escape. The trip to the falls takes you through the beautiful Grenadian open country.

6. Belmont Domain: For a sample of Grenada's flavor legacy, visit Belmont Bequest, a functioning ranch that offers direct visits where you can find out about cocoa, nutmeg, and other flavors' development and handling.

7. Nature Center at La Sagesse: Situated on the southeastern coast, this nature hold joins a shocking ocean side with mangrove backwoods and wetlands, giving a safe house to birdwatching and eco-the travel industry lovers.

8. Carriacou and Modest Martinique: These sister islands offer a more peaceful and easygoing experience, with delightful sea shores, brilliant coral reefs for jumping, and a brief look into the customary Grenadian lifestyle.

9. Levera Public Park: This safeguarded region on Grenada's northern coast is known for its different birdlife and settling reason for leatherback turtles. It's an incredible spot for nature sweethearts and untamed life lovers.

10. Grenada Chocolate Organization: In the event that you're a chocolate darling, don't miss a visit to the Grenada Chocolate Organization. They produce natural, tree-to-bar chocolate utilizing privately developed cocoa, offering a one of a kind and tasty experience.

Grenada's attractions offer an ideal mix of regular marvels, social encounters, and chances to loosen up in the quiet Caribbean environmental factors. Whether you're looking for experience or unwinding, Grenada has something for everybody to appreciate.

Things To Do And See In Grenada

The best things to do and see in Grenada are as follows:

Excellent Anse Beach: This is the most famous ocean side in Grenada, and for good explanation. It's an extended length of white sand with quiet, clear waters. There are a lot of retreats and cafés close by, so you can without much of a stretch go through an entire day here.

Seven Sisters Falls: These cascades are situated in the rainforest of the Amazing Etang Public Park. You can climb to the highest point of the succumbs to shocking perspectives, or take a dunk in the reviving pools at the base.

Rum Distillery: River Antoine Estate This rum refinery has been in activity starting around 1785. You can take a visit through the refinery and find out about the rum-production process. What's more, obviously, you can test a portion of the rum toward the finish of the visit.

Grenada Zest Gardens: This professional flowerbed is home to more than 400 types of flavors, including nutmeg, cinnamon, and cloves. You can take a directed visit through the nurseries and find out about the historical backdrop of flavors in Grenada.

Post George: This eighteenth century post offers shocking perspectives on St. George's. You can investigate the post's defenses and prisons, or basically loosen up on the grounds and partake in the perspectives.

Submerged Model Park: This novel park is situated off the shoreline of Grenada. It's home to more than 65 submerged models, which have turned into a well known spot for scuba jumping and swimming.

Dive and snorkeling: Grenada's reasonable waters are home to an assortment of marine life, making it an extraordinary spot for swimming and plunging. The Grand Etang Marine Reserve and the Molinere Underwater Sculpture Park are two of the island's many dive spots.

Hiking: Grenada is home to a few climbing trails, going from simple to testing. A few well known trails incorporate the Fabulous Etang Public Park Trail, the Harmony Falls Trail, and the Seven Sisters Falls Trail.

Culinary experiences: Grenada is known for its heavenly food, which is impacted by its Caribbean, French, and African legacy. Make certain to attempt a portion of the neighborhood dishes, for example, nutmeg gratin, callaloo, and oildown.

Outdoor Activities In Grenada

Grenada offers an abundance of outside exercises, because of its shocking normal scenes and warm environment. Here are a few famous open air pursuits on the island:

1. Ocean Side Experiences: With its flawless sea shores, Grenada is ideally suited for sunbathing, swimming, swimming, and jumping. Great Anse Ocean side, Morne Rouge Ocean side, and Levera Ocean side are among the top choices.

2. Hiking: Numerous trails on the island offer breathtaking views, making it a haven for hikers. Take on the difficult climb up Mount Holy Person Catherine or investigate the Annandale Cascades and Seven Sisters Cascades.

3. Water Sports: Partake in a scope of water sports, including kayaking, paddleboarding, and cruising.

The quiet, clear waters are great for amateurs and aficionados the same.

4. Scuba Jumping: Grenada is home to a variety of energetic coral reefs and wrecks, making it a superb objective for scuba jumpers. The submerged model park is a remarkable fascination worth investigating.

5. Plantations of spices: Leave on a visit through the island's flavor ranches, like nutmeg, cinnamon, and cocoa ranches. It's a potential chance to find out about Grenada's rich farming legacy.

6. Stream Tubing: Make a beeline for the Balthazar Stream or the Rail Waterway for an interesting waterway tubing experience, skimming down delicate rapids encompassed by rich tropical views.

7. Whale and Dolphin Watching: Take a boat visit to recognize great humpback whales or lively dolphins, particularly during their relocation seasons.

8. Jeep Safaris: Take a jeep safari tour into the island's interior to see waterfalls, rainforests, and other less-known attractions.

9. Cruising and Boat Sanctions: Contract a boat or join a cruising outing to investigate Grenada's close by islands, like Carriacou and Unimposing Martinique.

10. Birdwatching: Grenada is a haven for birdwatchers with north of 170 bird species. Make a beeline for the Fabulous Etang Public Park and Backwoods Save to detect brilliant local birds.

Make sure to regard the regular habitat and adhere to rules to save Grenada's perfect excellence while partaking in these open air exercises.

Shopping and Souvenirs In Grenada

Here are a few thoughts for shopping and keepsakes in Grenada:

Spices: Grenada is known as the "Spice Isle," so obviously you'll need to bring back certain flavors. Spices like nutmeg, ginger, cinnamon, and all spices are available in markets, stores, and even on the street.

Chocolate: Grenada additionally delivers scrumptious chocolate, produced using privately developed cocoa beans. You can track down chocolate bars, truffles, and different treats in many shops.

Handmade items: There are numerous capable craftsmen in Grenada who make lovely high quality things, for example, batik clothing, stoneware, gems, and woodwork.

Ocean glass: Grenada's sea shores are home to wonderful ocean glass, which is made when shells and different articles are separated by the sea. You can find ocean glass adornments, wind rings, and different trinkets produced using ocean glass.

Clothing: There are many shops in Grenada selling customary Caribbean clothing, like splendidly shaded dresses, shirts, and caps.

Music: Grenada has a rich melodic custom, and you can track down various melodic trinkets, like Cds, drums, and instruments.

Here are a few spots to go out to shop in Grenada:

Grand Anse Craft and Spice Market: On Grand Anse Beach, there is a huge market where you can buy clothing, spices, and other handicrafts as well as a wide range of souvenirs.

Spiceland Shopping center International: This is an enormous shopping center situated in Great Anse, with various stores, including obligation free shops, grocery stores, and shops.

Esplanade Mall: In St. George's, there is a small mall with a few shops that sell jewelry, clothing, and souvenirs.

Nutmeg Row: Spices, handicrafts, and other souvenirs can be found lined this street in St. George's.

Popular Shopping Areas In Grenada

Here are some famous shopping regions in Grenada:

In St. George's, there is a large shopping mall called "Spiceland Mall International." It has a wide assortment of stores, including clothing, keepsakes, gadgets, and food.

Excellent Anse Shopping Center is a more modest mall situated in Fantastic Anse. It is a popular destination for tourists to purchase beachwear and souvenirs due to its more laid-back atmosphere than Spiceland Mall.

Esplanade Shopping center Courtyard is a passerby just shopping region situated in St. George's. Numerous shops, restaurants, and bars can be found there.

St. George's has a waterfront shopping district called "Somers Wharf." It is a well known spot for travelers to purchase gifts, crafted works, and new fish.

The Specialty Market is an enormous outdoors market situated in St. George's. It is an extraordinary spot to find privately made gifts, handiworks, and flavors.

These are only a couple of the numerous well known shopping regions in Grenada. Regardless of what you are searching for, you make certain to track down it in one of these extraordinary spots.

Local Products and Souvenirs

Grenada's culture and natural resources are reflected in a wide range of local goods and souvenirs. A few well known things include:

1. Spices: Grenada is known as the "Flavor Isle," and you can track down excellent nutmeg, cinnamon, cloves, and different flavors.

2. Chocolate: Grenada produces a wide range of chocolate products, including delectable cocoa beans.

3. Rum: There are a variety of local rum brands and flavors because the island is also known for its rum.

4. Carefully assembled creates: Search for privately created things like woven bins, ceramics, and wood carvings.

5. Batik textures: Extraordinary batik textures and dresses are made utilizing conventional coloring strategies.

6. Jewelry: A few shops offer delightful gems made with neighborhood gemstones.

7. Artwork: Works of art and craftsmanship from Grenadian specialists are extraordinary gifts.

8. Nutmeg-related items: Besides flavors, you can find nutmeg-based items like oils, cleansers, and creams.

Make sure to help nearby craftsmen and organizations while buying these keepsakes. Blissful shopping!

Entertainment And Nightlife In Grenada.

Grenada has a genuinely tranquil nightlife, particularly when contrasted with different islands in the Caribbean. Nevertheless, there are still a few places to have a good time.

Here are probably the most well known nightlife spots in Grenada:

Fantazia Nightclub is the biggest and most well known club in Grenada. It's situated in St. George's and elements a wide assortment of music, from soca to reggae to dancehall.

Esther's Bar is a well known spot for local people and travelers. It has live music on weekends and is in Grand Anse. It has a casual atmosphere.

The Lime is a roof bar with dazzling perspectives on St. George's. It's an extraordinary spot to go for beverages and mingling.

The Rum Barrel is a well known rum bar in St. George's. They have a wide assortment of rums to browse and unrecorded music at the end of the week.

In Grand Anse, there is a beach bar called **"The Boatyard."** It's an incredible spot to go for beverages, food, and unrecorded music.

In the event that you're searching for something somewhat calmer, there are likewise various bars and eateries that have unrecorded music at the end of the week. These include:

- **The Lazy Lizard**

- **The Barbecue** at Spice Island Ocean side Resort

- **The Sundowner**

- **The Wreck Bar**

Regardless of what your taste is, you're certain to track down something to appreciate in Grenada's nightlife scene.

Best Beaches And Resorts In Grenada

Here are the absolute best sea shores and resorts in Grenada:

Fabulous Anse Beach: This is the most famous ocean side in Grenada, and for good explanation. It's a long, white-sand ocean side with quiet, clear waters. There are a lot of hotels and cafés along the ocean side, so you can without much of a stretch find all that you want.

Spear aux Epines Beach: This is one more well known ocean side in Grenada, found only north of Stupendous Anse Ocean side. It's undeniably calmer than Excellent Anse, yet it's as yet an incredible spot to unwind and partake in the sun and sand.

Pink Beach: This beach can be found just off the Grenada coast on the island of Carriacou. It's named for its pink sand, which is brought about by minute creatures that live in the water.

The Loch Muirhead: Grenada's southwest is home to this stunning lagoon. It's an incredible spot to swim, snorkel, or kayak. You can easily stay close to the action because there are a few resorts near the lagoon.

Zest Island Ocean side Resort: This comprehensive retreat is situated on the Stupendous Anse Ocean side. It has various cafés, bars, and exercises, so you can undoubtedly remain engaged.

Mount Cinnamon Inn and Ocean Side Club: This retreat is situated on the west bank of Grenada, sitting above the Great Anse Ocean side. It has various rooms and suites, as well as a spa, a wellness community, and different eateries.

Sandals in Grenada: This comprehensive retreat is situated on the southwest shoreline of Grenada. It has 10 cafés, 6 bars, 4 pools, and a spa.

These are only a couple of the numerous extraordinary sea shores and resorts in Grenada. With its lovely sea shores, rich rainforests, and well disposed individuals, Grenada is an incredible spot to unwind and partake in the Caribbean sun.

Chapter 3: Cultural and Culinary Experiences

Grenada's rich history and diverse heritage are at the heart of its cultural experiences. Festivals and events on the island showcase the island's vibrant traditions and customs. The most conspicuous comprehensive development is Amusement Park, held every year in August, highlighting energetic processions, calypso rivalries, and customary disguise exhibitions.

The captivating musical styles of the Grenadian people, such as calypso, soca, reggae, and steelpan, demonstrate their love of music. Local people and guests can appreciate live exhibitions in neighborhood settings or during unique occasions over time.

The island's design is a mix of pilgrim impacts and conventional Caribbean styles. Investigating St. George's, the capital city, uncovers vivid structures, memorable fortifications, and enchanting roads that offer a brief look into Grenada's past.

Grenada's culinary experiences are just as enticing, and the island's name, "Spice Isle," is a fitting description of its flavorful cuisine. The utilization of fragrant flavors like nutmeg, cinnamon, and turmeric adds an extraordinary turn to the neighborhood food.

Oil Down is Grenada's public dish and a must-pursue for guests. This good one-pot dinner incorporates breadfruit, salted meat or fish, coconut milk, callaloo (mixed greens), and different vegetables, stewed together to make a rich and heavenly flavor.

Fish assumes a critical part in Grenadian cooking, with top picks like barbecued lobster, fish stew, and shrimp dishes gracing the menus of numerous cafés. Nearby anglers guarantee that the fish is new and economically obtained.

Grenada is likewise known for its adoration for new natural products, for example, mangoes, papayas, pineapples, and soursops. Guests can enjoy invigorating organic product juices, smoothies, and natural product servings of mixed greens at nearby restaurants and road merchants.

For those with a sweet tooth, Grenadian pastries will not dishearten. Among the island's specialities that are sure to please any dessert lover are nutmeg ice cream and chocolate treats made from cacao grown locally.

A delightful way to immerse yourself in the island's flavors is to try local beverages like the well-known "Rivers" rum and freshly squeezed nutmeg-infused drinks.

Generally, Grenada's social and culinary encounters offer a dazzling excursion through its legacy, leaving guests with extraordinary recollections and a more profound appreciation for the island's special personality.

Culture And Traditions Of Grenada

Grenada's way of life and customs are a captivating mix of African, European, and native impacts, molded by its set of experiences and different legacies. Here are a few critical parts of Grenada's way of life and customs:

1. Music and Dance: Grenadian music is a big part of their culture, and you'll often hear steelpan, calypso, soca, and reggae with their lively rhythms. Festivals like Carnival and other celebrations feature a lot of these genres. Conventional dance structures, like the Quadrille and Bele, are additionally esteemed and performed on unique events.

2. Carnival: Amusement park is perhaps the main far-reaching development in Grenada, celebrated every year in August. Exquisite parades, masquerade bands, calypso competitions, and a variety of cultural displays make up this vibrant and colorful festival. Locals and visitors alike are brought together during this time of celebration and joy.

3. Language: Grenada's official language is English, but locals may speak "Grenadian Creole" or "Patois," a Creole language. This language is a blend of English, African dialects, and French, and it features the island's phonetic variety.

4. Architecture: Grenada's design mirrors its set of experiences of colonization and the mixing of societies. The island's traditional wooden homes and colorful buildings, as well as its historic structures like Fort George and Fort Frederick, add charm to the towns and villages.

5. Cuisine: Grenadian food is a great combination of flavors and flavors. The plentiful utilization of flavors like nutmeg, cinnamon, and cloves procured

Grenada the moniker "Zest Isle." Neighborhood dishes like Oil Down (one-pot dinner), Callaloo (mixed greens stew), and different fish treats feature the island's culinary variety.

6. Fishing and Agribusiness: Fishing and agribusiness are necessary to Grenadian culture and customs. The fishing business is huge, with nearby anglers providing new fish to business sectors and cafés. The island's lavish scene upholds horticulture, with nutmeg, cocoa, and different flavors being fundamental products.

7. Stories and Folklore: Grenadian legends and narrating make light of a job in passing social convictions and customs. Stories of legendary animals like La Diablesse and accounts of familial spirits are divided between ages, adding a feeling of secret and charm to the island's way of life.

8. Traditions and Celebrations: Close by Fair, Grenadians celebrate different strict and social occasions, like Easter, Christmas, and Liberation Day. Family get-togethers and shared festivals are necessary to the island's social texture.

9. Regard for Nature: Grenadians have a profound association with their regular environmental elements. The island's beautiful beaches, lush rainforests, and waterfalls are regarded as sacred, and there is a strong focus on protecting the environment for future generations.

These social components, alongside the warm and inviting nature of the Grenadian public, make an interesting and enthralling social embroidery that has an enduring effect on anybody sufficiently lucky to encounter it.

Festivals and Events In Grenada

Grenada has different lively celebrations and occasions over time, mirroring the island's rich social legacy and customs. Here are probably the most remarkable celebrations and occasions in Grenada:

1. Carnival: Grenada's Amusement park, otherwise called "Spicemas," is the feature of the island's occasions schedule. Celebrated in August, the Fair is an energetic scene highlighting beautiful processions, calypso rivalries, steelpan music, and conventional disguise exhibitions. It is a period of happiness, party, and social articulations.

2. Grenada Cruising Celebration: Held in January or February, the Grenada Cruising Celebration exhibits the island's marine legacy. The occasion highlights different cruising races, including the completely exhilarating Work Boat Regatta, which sees nearby anglers handily hustling their conventional wooden boats.

3. Grenada Chocolate Fest: Chocolate darlings shouldn't miss this heavenly occasion in May. The Grenada Chocolate Fest praises the island's cacao legacy, offering chocolate tastings, studios, and voyages through neighborhood cocoa ranches and chocolate processing plants.

4. Carriacou Maroon and String Band Live performance: The sister island of Carriacou plays host to this one-of-a-kind festival in April. It features cultural displays, traditional drumming, string band music, and a celebration of the island's African heritage.

5. Angler's Birthday Festivities: Known as Angler's Birthday, this occasion in June honors the island's fishing local area. Merriments incorporate boat races, fishing rivalries, and a lively road party.

6. Unadulterated Grenada Live concert: Music lovers will partake in this yearly live event held in April or May. The occasion features neighborhood and worldwide specialists, offering a different scope of melodic classifications for participants to appreciate.

7. Carriacou Amusement Park: Carriacou's form of Festival happens in February or Walk, highlighting brilliant processions, calypso contests, and conventional disguise exhibitions. It offers a more cozy and genuine Fair experience contrasted with the headliner on the principal island of Grenada.

8. Freedom Day: Celebrated on February seventh, Freedom Day recognizes Grenada acquiring autonomy from English rule in 1974. The island wakes up with social presentations, banner raising services, marches, and vivacious celebrations.

9. Liberation Day: Celebrated on August first, Liberation Day respects the nullification of subjection in the English settlements. It is set apart with services, social exhibitions, and occasions that ponder the island's set of experiences and opportunities.

Grenada's vibrancy, diversity, and cultural richness are on display at these festivals and events, which offer visitors and residents alike an unforgettable experience.

Grenada Foods And Drinks You May Try

The island's abundance of spices and fresh ingredients have influenced Grenada's cuisine, which is a delightful fusion of flavors. While visiting Grenada, make a point to enjoy these flavorful food varieties and beverages:

Oil Down: This is the public dish of Grenada and is a good stew made with meat, dumplings, vegetables, and coconut milk. It is a delectable and satiating dish that is typically prepared over an open fire.

Roti: This is a sort of flatbread that is frequently loaded up with curried meat, vegetables, or cheddar. It's a popular Grenada street food that lets you try a variety of flavors.

Callaloo Soup: This is a thick soup made with callaloo leaves, okra, and different vegetables. It is frequently presented with dumplings or bread and is a famous breakfast or lunch dish.

Nutmeg Ice Cream: Nutmeg ice cream is a popular dessert in Grenada because the island produces the most nutmeg in the world. The frozen yogurt is made with new nutmeg and is a flavorful and reviving method for chilling on a hot day.

'Curried Goat:' This is a famous dish in the Caribbean and is made with goat meat that is slow-cooked in a curry sauce. It is commonly presented with rice and peas or roti.

Lambie Souse: This is a customary Grenadian dish made with cured conch. It is somewhat of a mixed bag, yet the individuals who love it depend on it.

Broiled Prepare and Saltfish: This is a straightforward however tasty dish that is made with broiled preparations (flatbreads) and saltfish (dried, salted cod). It is frequently presented with a side of hot sauce or pepper sauce.

Chocolate: Grenada is likewise known for its chocolate, so make certain to attempt some while you are on the island. There are various chocolate production lines on the island where you can test various sorts of chocolate and find out about the chocolate-production process.

Coming up next are probably the best beverages you ought to attempt in Grenada:

Rum Punch: This is the mark drink of Grenada and is made with rum, organic product squeezes, and flavors. It is regularly presented with a float of nutmeg and is a delectable and reviving method for partaking in the island's rum.

Coconut tea: This is a hot beverage made with cocoa powder, nutmeg, and sugar. It is a famous beverage in the first part of the day or night and is a scrumptious method for heating up.

Grenadine Swizzle: This is a reviving mixed drink made with grenadine, rum, lime juice, and Angostura sharp flavoring. It is commonly presented with a branch of mint and is an incredible method for chilling on a hot day.

Waterway Antoine Rum: This is a rum delivered at the Waterway Antoine Bequest, which is perhaps the most established refinery in the Caribbean. The rum is produced using sugarcane that is developed at home and is known for its smooth and tasty taste.

Carib Beer: This is a nearby lager that is prepared in Grenada. An invigorating and simple drinking lager is ideal for getting a charge out of on the ocean front or at a bar.

I want to believe that you partake in your outing to Grenada and attempt a portion of these scrumptious food varieties and beverages!

Local Markets And Street Food

Here are a portion of the neighborhood market and road food sources you can track down in Grenada:

Doubles: This is a famous road food in Grenada that started in Trinidad and Tobago. It is made with two bits of bara, a level broiled bread made of flour, baking powder, and turmeric, loaded down with somewhat hot curried chickpeas. It is frequently finished off with sweet mango and hot pepper.

Roti: This is a wrap made with a flatbread called paratha, loaded up with different fixings, like curried chickpeas, meat, or vegetables. It is a well known breakfast or lunch choice in Grenada.

Jerk chicken: This is a kind of grilled chicken that is marinated in a mix of flavors, including scotch hood peppers, allspice, and thyme. It is a famous dish in Grenada and all through the Caribbean.

Oil down: This is Grenada's public dish. It is a stew made with meat, vegetables, and flavors, and it is cooked in coconut milk. A generous and tasty dish is normally served at extraordinary events.

Pholourie: This is a seared cake made with chickpea flour. It is frequently loaded up with curried chickpeas, meat, or vegetables. It is a famous road food in Grenada and all through the Caribbean.

Seafood: Grenada is an island, so fish is a famous dish. You can find an assortment of fish dishes in Grenada, including barbecued fish, lobster, and conch.

These are only a couple of the numerous nearby market and road food sources you can track down in Grenada. On the off chance that you are searching for a flavorful and real taste of Grenada, make certain to attempt a portion of these dishes.

Here are a portion of the spots where you can track down these road food sources in Grenada:

Market Square: This is the primary market in St. George's, Grenada. You will find different stores selling nearby produce, flavors, and keepsakes. There are likewise a couple of foods that slows down selling road food, like duplicates, roti, and pholourie.

Terrific Anse Beach: This is quite possibly the most well known ocean side in Grenada. There are various eateries and restaurants along the ocean side that sell road food, like jerk chicken, fish, and roti.

Spiceland Mall: This is a shopping center in St. George's has various food stores selling road food, like duplicates, roti, and pholourie.

Best Restaurants In Grenada

Here are the absolute best cafés in Grenada, as per Tripadvisor:

Dodgy Dock Restaurant is a relaxed beachside café with an exuberant climate. It serves an assortment of Caribbean dishes, including new fish, rotis, and jerk chicken.

Rhodes Café at Calabash is a fancy eatery with dazzling perspectives on Fabulous Anse Ocean side. The menu highlights current Caribbean cooking with an emphasis on new, nearby fixings.

Patrick's Nearby Homestyle Restaurant is an extraordinary spot to attempt conventional Grenadian food. The menu highlights dishes like oil down, seared prepare and saltfish, and lambie immerse.

Carib Sushi is a well known spot for sushi and Japanese food. The café has a casual environment and a wide assortment of rolls to look over.

The First Slipway is a waterfront eatery with an emphasis on fish. The menu includes new fish got day to day, as well as lobster and other barbecued dishes.

Here are some other profoundly evaluated cafés in Grenada:

- Armadillo Eatery
- The Ocean Side Club at Calabash
- Butch's Chophouse
- Bogles Round House
- Sails Eatery and Bar
- Free Bar and Barbecue
- BB's Crabback
- Kayak Kafe and Juice Bar
- Laluna Eatery

These are only a couple of the numerous extraordinary eateries in Grenada. Regardless of what your taste, you're certain to track down something however you would prefer

Useful Phrases And Vocabulary

Here are a few valuable Grenadian Creole expressions and jargon:

1. Bonjou - Good day
2. Bonswa - Goodbye
3. Mèsi - Bless your heart
4. Ki jan ou rele? - What is your name?
5. Mwen rele... - My name is...
6. Kijan ou ye? - How are you?
7. Mwen byen - I'm fine
8. Wi - Yes
9. Non - No
10. Dad gen pwoblem - No issue
11. Kisa ou vle? - What is it that you need?
12. Kote mwen ka jwenn...? - Where can I find...?
13. Kijan mwen ka ale...? - How might I go...?
14. Kòman ou di sa a Kreyol? - How would you express that in Creole?
15. Anvi manje - I need to eat
16. Mwen renmen manje - I love food
17. Anvi beer - I need to go
18. Kisa sa vle di? - What's the significance here?
19. Ou ka pale pi dousman? - Might you at any point talk all the more leisurely?

20. Mwen dad konprann - I don't have the foggiest idea
21. Dlo - Water
22. Manje - Food
23. Kaz - House
24. Machwè - Ocean side
25. Lapli - Downpour
26. Solèy - Sun

Recall that Grenadian Creole, similar to some other creole language, could shift in various districts or networks. These expressions ought to furnish you with a decent beginning stage for essential correspondence. Cheerful learning!

Chapter 4: Practical Information

Grenada is a Caribbean country known for its shocking sea shores, lavish scenes, and dynamic culture. Here is some functional data:

1. Location: Grenada is situated in the southeastern Caribbean Ocean, northwest of Trinidad and Tobago.

2. Capital: The capital city is St. George's.

3. Language: English is the authority language.

4. Currency: The Eastern Caribbean Dollar (XCD) is the authority money.

5.Time Zone: Grenada keeps Atlantic Guideline Time (AST), which is UTC-4.

6. Passage Requirements: Actually take a look at the most recent visa and passage necessities prior to voyaging. A substantial visa is normally required.

7. Climate: Grenada has a heat and humidity, with a dry season from January to May and a stormy season from June to December. Normal temperatures range from 77-88°F (25-31°C).

8. Wellbeing and Safety: It's prescribed to have forward-thinking inoculations and convey mosquito repellent to safeguard against mosquito-borne sicknesses. The regular water is for the most part protected to drink.

9. Transportation: Public transportation choices incorporate transports and shared taxis. Leasing a vehicle is likewise a helpful method for investigating the island.

10. Electricity: The standard voltage is 230V, and the essential attachment type will be Type G, like the UK.

11. Cuisine: Grenadian food includes a blend of Caribbean and Creole flavors. Try not to miss attempting dishes like "oil down" (a good one-pot dinner) and new fish.

12. Attractions: Famous attractions incorporate Fabulous Anse Ocean side, St. George's Market, Post George, and the Annandale Cascade.

13. Cash Exchange: Cash can be traded at banks, trade departments, or lodgings.

14. Communication: The nation code for worldwide calls to Grenada is +1-473.

15. Internet: Most facilities and public spots offer Wi-Fi access.

Recollect that this data could change after some time, so it's consistently smart to twofold check with true sources or your travel service before your excursion.

Safety Tips And Precautions

Security tips and safeguards in Grenada include:

1. Remain mindful of your environmental factors and stay away from dreary or segregated regions, particularly around evening time.

2. Secure your possessions and try not to show resources out in the open to stop robbery.

3. Utilize authorized taxis or respectable transportation administrations while moving around the island.

4. Regard neighborhood customs and customs, as well as nearby regulations and guidelines.

5. Be careful while swimming in new waters and focus on advance notice banners on sea shores.

6. Remain refreshed on weather patterns and potential normal risks like typhoons or weighty precipitation.

7. Hydrate and try not to polish off untreated faucet water to forestall waterborne diseases.

8. Convey a duplicate of your recognizable proof and travel reports, while keeping the firsts in a solid area.

9. Be mindful while partaking in water sports or trips and guarantee they are driven by experienced guides.

10. Assuming that you intend to climb or investigate nature, advise somebody regarding your arrangements and take vital supplies with you.

Keep in mind, being educated and utilizing good judgment is vital to guaranteeing a protected and charming involvement with Grenada.

Health Considerations

Prosperity examinations in Grenada twirl around ensuring your thriving during your visit on the island. The following are a couple of focal issues to recollect:

1. Clinical Facilities: Grenada has crisis centers and clinical offices, particularly in the foremost towns like St. George's. While the clinical consideration structure is adequate, having travel assurance that takes care of clinical costs in case of ailment or injury is major.

2.Vaccinations: Before making an outing to Grenada, check with your clinical benefits provider or a development prosperity office to promise you are in the loop in regards to routine vaccinations. Dependent upon your development history and plans, certain additional vaccinations may be proposed, so talk with a clinical consideration capable.

3. Mosquito-Borne Illnesses: Grenada, as other Caribbean countries, is frail to mosquito-borne diseases like Zika, Dengue, and Chikungunya. Defend yourself by using bug enemies of specialists, wearing long-sleeved dresses, and staying in offices with screens or cooling.

4. Sun Exposure: The intensity and mugginess in Grenada can be exceptionally boiling, so it's crucial to stay hydrated and use sunscreen with a high SPF to protect yourself from the sun's destructive bars.

5. Food and Water Safety: While spigot water is generally safeguarded to drink in Grenada, a couple of visitors favor sifted water. While eating at neighborhood diners, ensure that the food is completely cooked and served hot. Be aware of fish and simply eat from authentic establishments.

6. Clinical Insurance: As a visitor, having comprehensive travel clinical security is pressing to cover any frightening wellbeing related emergencies or bringing back.

7. Covid Precautions: Dependent upon the continuous situation, there may be express Covid rules and constraints set up. Stay informed about the latest updates from neighboring subject matter experts and adhere to any security implications.

8. **Specialist recommended Medications:** Expecting that you require doctor suggested prescriptions, promise you have a palatable stock

for whatever length of time your visit would endure. Convey them in their novel compartments and convey a copy of your answer with you.

9. Emergency Services: Learn about the local emergency organization's number (911 in Grenada) and know the region of the nearest center or clinical office.

10. Individual Health: Manage your prosperity by staying aware of incredible tidiness, getting adequate rest, and avoiding extreme alcohol use.

By being proactive and mindful of your prosperity during your time in Grenada, you can totally participate in the greatness and experiences the island offers of real value. Make a point to chat with clinical benefits capable before your trip to address specific prosperity concerns you could have.

Local Customs And Etiquette

Traditions and decorum assume a critical part in the dynamic culture of Grenada. Here are a few significant perspectives to remember:

1. Good tidings and Politeness: Grenadians esteem pleasantness and neighborliness. Welcoming individuals with a comforting grin and a well disposed "Hello" or "Great afternoon is standard." Utilizing titles like Mr., Mrs., or Miss while tending to somebody, trailed by their last name, is thought of as deferential.

2. Gift-Giving: When welcome to somebody's house, it's an act of kindness to bring a little gift as a badge of appreciation. This could be a bunch of roses, a crate of chocolates, or a privately made trinket. This signal mirrors your appreciation and generosity.

3. Handshakes and Gestures: While saying hello to somebody, utilize your right hand for handshakes or signals. The left hand is customarily viewed as less spotless and is best kept away from conventional communications.

4. Eating Etiquette: While feasting with local people, it's well mannered to trust that the host will begin eating before you start. Finish all the food on your plate as a noble gesture for the feast and the work put into setting it up. In the event that you're a visitor, communicating appreciation for the food is a gracious motion.

5. Dress Code: While beachwear is appropriate for the ocean side, dressing unassumingly around and in public places is significant. Uncovering or excessively relaxed clothing might be viewed as rude. Wearing proper attire shows thought for nearby traditions.

6. Photography and Regard for Privacy: Continuously request consent prior to taking photographs of local people or their property. Regarding their security and culture is considerate. While visiting strict destinations or widespread developments, observe any rules or rules given by local people.

7. Regard for Strict Locales and Traditions: Grenada has a different strict scene, including Christianity, Hinduism, and Islam. While visiting holy places, sanctuaries, or other strict destinations, be aware of the traditions and practices seen there.

8. Language and Communication: English is the authority language in Grenada, and it's vital to impart it obviously and consciously. Participate in discussions with interest and amiability, considering authentic associations with local people.

9. Public Behavior: Show thought for others by keeping a conscious and obliging disposition openly. Noisy or problematic ways of behaving may be seen adversely, as Grenadians put areas of strength for local areas and agreeable communications.

10. Cooperation in Neighborhood Traditions: On the off chance that you have the chance to take part in neighborhood festivities, celebrations, or customs, embrace the involvement with a receptive outlook and an eagerness to learn. Participating in these practices encourages a more profound comprehension and enthusiasm for Grenadian culture.

By noticing these neighborhood customs and rehearsing great decorum, you'll have the option to associate all the more definitively with individuals of Grenada and contribute decidedly to your social encounters on the island.

Currency And Money Matters

The authority money of Grenada is the Eastern Caribbean Dollar (EC$), which is fixed to the US dollar at a pace of EC$2.70 = US$1.00. This implies that US dollars are acknowledged as lawful delicate in Grenada, and can be traded for Eastern Caribbean dollars at banks and trade departments. Notwithstanding, it is normally best to trade your money for Eastern Caribbean dollars before you show up in Grenada, as you will get a superior conversion scale.

There are seven groups of Eastern Caribbean dollars: $1, $2, $5, $10, $20, $50, and $100 notes. Coins are as of now not available for use.

Banks in Grenada are open from Monday to Friday, from 8:30am to 4:30pm. Trade agencies are open longer hours, normally from 8:00am to 6:00pm, and some are open at the end of the week.

It is essential to take note that charge cards are not generally acknowledged in Grenada, so it is really smart to carry some money with you when you travel. You can likewise utilize your Mastercard at a few bigger inns and cafés, yet you might be charged an additional charge.

Here are a few ways to involve cash and cash in Grenada:

- Trade your money for Eastern Caribbean dollars before you show up in Grenada.

- Utilize your Visa at bigger lodgings and eateries, yet be ready to pay an extra charge.

- Convey some money with you, as Visas are not generally acknowledged.

- Know about the swapping scale while trading your cash.

- Keep your cash in a protected spot, for example, a cash belt or a protected one in your lodging.

- Report any lost or taken money to the police right away.

Time Zone and Public Holidays

Grenada notices Atlantic Standard Time (AST) throughout the entire year. This is 4 hours behind Facilitated General Time (UTC) or 1 hour in front of Eastern Standard Time (EST). There is no light saving time in Grenada.

Here are the public occasions in Grenada in 2023:

- New Year's Day (January 1)
- Great Friday (April 7)
- Easter Monday (April 10)
- Work Day (May 1)
- Sovereign's Birthday (June 12)

- Liberation Day (August 7)
- Festival (August 14-15)
- Autonomy Day (August 31)
- Christmas Day (December 25)
- Boxing Day (December 26)

If it's not too much trouble, note that these occasions might be dependent on future developments, so it is in every case best to check with the Grenada government site for the most state-of-the-art data.

Here are some extra things to remember in Grenada:

- The financial hours in Grenada are Monday to Friday from 8:00 AM to 3:00 PM.

- The shops in Grenada are by and large open from 9:00 AM to 6:00 PM, Monday to Saturday.

- There are various celebrations and occasions held in Grenada over time. These incorporate the Grenada Chocolate Celebration, the Zest Mas Celebration, and the Carriacou Regatta.

How To Save Money On Grenada Vacation

Setting aside cash during an excursion in Grenada, similar to some other travel objective, requires insightful preparation and savvy navigation. Here are a few hints to assist you with capitalizing on your outing while at the same time holding your costs under wraps:

1. Budgeting: Set an unmistakable financial plan for your excursion, framing the amount you're willing to spend on facilities, transportation, food, exercises, and keepsakes. Adhere to this spending plan to abstain from overspending.

2. Accommodations: Consider remaining in guesthouses, lodgings, or excursion rentals rather than lavish inns. Search for arrangements and limits, and consider booking facilities ahead of time to get lower rates.

3. Travel Timing: Go during the off-top seasons, which can assist you with saving money on flights, facilities, and exercises. Stay away from significant occasions and pinnacle vacationer months if conceivable.

4. Flight Deals: Look for flight arrangements and use admission correlation sites to track down the best costs. Be adaptable with your movement dates and think about flying on work days, as flights are frequently less expensive.

5. Nearby Transportation: Utilize public transportation, like transports and shared taxis, rather than costly confidential exchanges. Leasing a vehicle could be practical on the off chance that you intend to widely investigate the island.

6. Eating Economically: Appreciate nearby cooking and road food, which are many times more reasonable than feasting in upscale eateries. Think about purchasing food and setting up your very own portion feasts on the off chance that your facilities permit.

7. Water Activities: Rather than booking costly visits, explore and find reasonable or free exercises like swimming, swimming, or beachcombing.

8. Free Attractions: Investigate free or minimal expense attractions like climbing trails, public sea shores, and authentic destinations. Grenada offers dazzling normal magnificence that doesn't need a strong sticker price.

9. Nearby Markets: Shop at neighborhood markets for new produce, tidbits, and gifts. You can frequently track down extraordinary things at preferred costs over in touristy shops.

10. Cash Exchange: Be aware of money trade rates and charges. Pull out cash from ATMs in nearby money for better rates, and illuminate your bank about your itinerary items to stay away from any issues.

11. Try not to Wander Charges: To save money on correspondence costs, consider buying a neighborhood SIM card or utilizing free Wi-Fi accessible at numerous bistros and facilities.

12. Trinket Shopping: Search for legitimate, privately made trinkets at sensible costs. Try not to purchase gifts from touristy regions, where costs will more often than not be higher.

By carrying out these useful ways to save cash, you can partake in an important get-away in Grenada without burning through every last cent. Recall that being creative, exploring ahead of time, and going with cognizant spending decisions will add to a more reasonable and charming travel insight.

Do's And Don'ts In Grenada

Here are some do's and don'ts to remember while visiting Grenada:

Do:

- Visit the flavor ranches and find out about Grenada's set of experiences as the "Zest Island."

- Climb to the Seven Falls, a wonderful series of cascades in the rainforest.

- Go swimming or take a plunge into the reasonable waters around Grenada to see the beautiful coral reefs and fish.

- Go on a boat outing to the Submerged Model Park, an interesting submerged workmanship show.

- Loosen up on one of Grenada's numerous lovely sea shores, for example, Amazing Anse Ocean side or Spear aux Epines Ocean side.

- Test the nearby food, which is impacted by French, African, and Caribbean flavors.

- Make certain to attempt nutmeg, Grenada's public flavor!

Don't:
- Stroll around in swimwear in open regions. This is viewed as revolting openness and can get you fined.

- Be excessively tender openly. Grenada is a moderate nation and public presentations of fondness are disapproved of.

- Drink the faucet water. It isn't protected to drink the faucet water in Grenada, so make certain to hydrate all things considered.

- Buy gifts produced using jeopardized species, like tortoiseshell adornments or coral.

- Leave junk around the ocean or in the rainforest. Grenada is a wonderful nation and it is vital to assist with keeping it clean.

- Take photographs of individuals without their consent. This is viewed as discourteous in Grenada.

Generally, Grenada is a protected and cordial country with a great deal to offer guests. By following these do's and don'ts, you can guarantee that you live it up on your excursion.

Conclusion

All in all, Grenada offers an enamoring mix of staggering normal excellence, energetic culture, and warm friendliness that has an enduring impact on each explorer sufficiently lucky to visit. From its flawless sea shores and lavish rainforests to its notable locales and delightful food, Grenada is an objective that genuinely has something for everybody. Whether you look for unwinding, experience, or a more profound association with neighborhood customs, this charming island country guarantees an extraordinary excursion that will without a doubt wait in your heart and recollections into the indefinite future. So gather your sacks, drench yourself in Grenada's charms, and leave on a journey of disclosure that will without a doubt be carved in your movement story for eternity.

Made in the USA
Columbia, SC
04 November 2024

45654569R00052